D1049305

The Letters to Brave Heart

THE VIEW FROM THE CLEFT

Marcia Goranson

TRILOGY CHRISTIAN PUBLISHERS
Tustin, CA

Trilogy Christian Publishers

A Wholly Owned Subsidiary of Trinity Broadcasting Network

2442 Michelle Drive

Tustin, CA 92780

For information, address Trilogy Christian Publishing

Rights Department, 2442 Michelle Drive, Tustin, Ca 92780.

Trilogy Christian Publishing/ TBN and colophon are trademarks of Trinity Broadcasting Network.

For information about special discounts for bulk purchases, please contact Trilogy Christian Publishing.

Manufactured in the United States of America

10 9 8 7 6 5 4 3 2 1

Library of Congress Cataloging-in-Publication Data is available.

ISBN 978-1-64088-343-7

ISBN 978-1-64088-344-4 (ebook)

Contents

Foreword

Many years ago, when I had just begun my counseling career, the Lord entrusted me with Brave Heart. She had responded to the overwhelming call of God to find healing, whatever the cost. Marcia did not know yet that she was brave. She had no idea that the journey of her soul would ultimately lead her to find Brave Heart. She was completely unaware that she was getting ready to venture into the cleft where she would not only find healing, but also beckon others to heal. All she knew was she was collapsing under the weight of her abuse and her lifelong burden to keep it in the hidden sewer hole of shame and secrecy.

What a gift to encounter a heart like Marcia's. She loved the Lord deeply and desperately wanted to heal from the shackles that had kept her arrested for so long. She was ready to work, ready to face the deep, ready to do whatever it took to find the freedom for which Christ had come to set her free.

We began the work by laying her shame at the feet of Jesus. We took the pain, the grief, the loss of innocence and lack of validation to the Good Shepherd where He so faithfully and artfully ushered in healing, forgiveness, validation, and acceptance.

What an honor it was to walk her to the Throne of Grace at that time, and what a treasure it has been to live at the Throne with her. Since being reunited years later as she reached out to share her many victories, I urged her to make her story known. Through this process, Marcia has become a dear friend and confidant whom the Lord has used to bless my soul, as I am certain she will also bless yours.

Dear reader, it is my great pleasure to introduce you to a hero for healing, Brave Heart. May the Lord show you the tender mercies existing in His cleft, and may He provide courage to your soul that you may be brave and find the healing he came to give.

Anna Raab

Rock of Ages, cleft for me, let me hide myself in Thee...

—THOMAS HASTINGS

"Every block of stone has a statue inside it and it is the task of the sculptor to discover it."

—MICHELANGELO

Dedication

To the loves of my life- Mr G, Ms G and Jr. G. Also to Anna- thank you for the challenge, it's changed everything.

Letter One

Dear Beloved Reader,

This narrative is written to you and to young Brave Heart from my perspective, from my position, looking back almost 50 years. I am now Brave Heart, the author and Christ follower, who lives and thrives in "The Cleft", a safe, secure place my Heavenly Father opened for me, within Himself almost twenty years ago now. I'm sharing what has come to me, my point of view, while I have been in the process of healing, transforming and becoming more like Jesus Christ, the Good Shepherd and less like the marble statue where I lie hidden in the human condition, something I hold in common with each person. Brave Heart's story—my story—is about recovering the masterpiece that we were each intended to be. There is beauty and Christlikeness in every soul, in every life, from conception, from birth, a beauty that only a loving Creator could conceive of and masterfully sculpt and form.

As I, Brave Heart, share this perspective, this view, with the younger version of myself, you the Beloved Reader will gain an insight into my lifelong relationship with the Lover of my soul. Beginning in early childhood and reaching into eternity, this relationship was initiated by the source of pure, powerful love and received fully by my child's innocent Heart.

Around the age of seven or eight, there was an evil, insidious attempt to tarnish this relationship of gold--to hinder it, to destroy it. The actual physical acts of evil flung my childhood innocence to the dung heap, shattering my identity and forcing me into falsehood in order to cope and survive the residual effects. Wrong thinking and false believing and outright lies entered my mind where before there had been life and peace. I believed falsely that a chasm had been created between the Good Shepherd and myself because of the evil that had been inflicted on me. I believed that I belonged on the dark side of the divide, on the outer shore of His love, as far from His goodness that I could get.

As I said, my story is about recovery, restoration and uncovering the David, the masterpiece that lies within each of us. Writing this from within the Cleft, the place where I have healed, I have transformed from a limping victim to confident survivor and then to Overcomer who is now willing and able to share the truth. Telling the truth is the motivation for writing "The Letters." Telling the truth about love, shame and reconciliation. It is a story of how denying and ignoring the grittiness of sin and its effects causes deep pain in the life of every person. Mostly, Brave Heart's story reveals that the keeping of perverse, ancient secrets and vile family codes fertilizes the ground of dysfunction for a multitude of generations and results in stunting emotional health and renders mountains of human potential powerless.

The "Letters to Brave Heart" recounts my journey of coming to and reaching the Cleft, and the healing process that I found waiting there. Come along, Beloved Reader. Follow Brave Heart's story and find the open arms of the Good Shepherd, who is waiting for each of us, never not loving us.

The retrieval of the masterpiece hidden in the stone of the human condition, lies in the skilled hands of the Holy Spirit, the Helper, our Michelangelo. His purpose in transforming the marble into the likeness of the Good Shepherd is so that He, the Lord of Life, would be glorified and known to everyone. When I, Brave Heart entered the Cleft at forty-four years of age, my one goal was to find relief from the heartbreak that had been with me since childhood. As I entered the Cleft, a safe place that my Heavenly Father opened within Himself and fit me into, I said yes to the commencement of the sculpting of my soul. The initial pain of having the hardness of the marble in my soul chipped away lovingly, soon gave way to the relief and peace that came when I became friends finally with the Helper and willingly cooperated with Him. Not out of obligation or fear, but because I came to know and accept that He loves me with an unending, powerful love, which created trust.

Beloved Reader, what made the uniqueness of this transformation process remarkable was the continual course in *unlearning.* Unlearning all of the false things that I believed about the Good Shepherd and myself. Traditions, doubt, unbelief and the effects of many lies are all chipped away as I developed an awareness and acceptance of the truth about the Creator's eternal intentions for me. The goal of the recovery and restoration of the David in the marble is that everything that is not characteristic of or true to the character and image of the Good Shepherd will eventually fall off and fall away. The resolution of my pain came and continues to come through the layers of my humanity as more and more of the likeness of Jesus Christ replaces the hardness of the statue of stone. My continued friendship and cooperation with the Helper, the gentle, merciful third person of the Trinity, insures me that the truth will be lived out, that Christ will be glorified and I will become everything that He always intended me to be. We have all of Eternity after all.

These letters, Beloved Reader, sketch out the progress of Brave Heart's walk with the Good Shepherd, both outside of and inside the Cleft, which is a physical place and a spiritual place as well. The Cleft is in the 'Palm of His Hand', the Creator's hand or a space in Himself that He created for Brave Heart. He placed her there. There is no way into or out of the Cleft unless He puts His child there or removes them. It is a safe place in Him...its not restrictive but protective. He placed Brave Heart there at her request. It's a place to heal and to grow. There is room for the Helper to do His sculpting work. It's an eternal haven now. It was a refuge from the pain at first but now it's the place where Brave Heart will always live. His goal for her is eternal and eternity began for her when she first knew and loved the Good Shepherd, her Savior, as a child.

Beloved Reader, Brave Heart's story is true and it is written for you. It is the truth about how she lived with and dealt with and denied trauma and effects left unprocessed. Her pain is not unique or uncommon but it is deep and multi-layered. Everyone experiences trauma, difficult or tragic times in the course of a lifetime. The difference in her story is the redemption of her pain that comes only after she enters the Cleft and befriends the Helper, the Holy Spirit, and the actual presence of God in the Earth.

The only strength Brave Heart had in and of herself was the power of resistance, which is also common to everyone and it is what was modeled to her as a coping mechanism from the beginning of her life. Instead of acknowledging the trauma, the pain and its effects, she attempted to ignore it and bury it alive to keep it secret.

The strong thread in Brave Heart's story is how the love of the Good Shepherd, Jesus Christ, and the strength of her resistance, her own power, met head on and what the outcome of that collision was. The love and forbearance is another consistent thread in the Letters. This love isn't just what He does; it's who He is. Unwavering and persistent, yet calm and patient. Once we belong to Him, dear Reader, He will never let us go. (John 10:28)

We are so precious to Him, Dear Reader, that He will never turn away from us, even and especially in the face of our pain, shame, rebellion, self-righteousness, drunkenness, promiscuity or any other self-destructive device or method.

Our lives on Earth are meant to be 70 or 80 years of preparation for eternity, Precious Reader. When we give our hearts and lives to Him fully and in love, He will spend our earthly lifetimes teaching us how to love Him foremost and then how to love others as we love ourselves. Find your life in Jesus Christ, Dear Reader. Allow yourself to be conformed to His image, His likeness. Knowing Him intimately will cause you to fall so deeply in love with Him. He is the most infinitely awesome Person in the Universe. You will never regret, Precious One, making the choice to believe Him, trust Him and to follow Him into true freedom because knowing Him IS true freedom. (John 17:3)

The deepest part of each soul longs to become like Him after we ask Him to be the Lord of our lives and He becomes the object of our attention and focus. Our re-created hearts long to resemble the Good Shepherd because we love Him and He is the truth in our lives.

This is in essence, the heart of Brave Heart's journey from a fractured and broken child who loved the Lord from her earliest memory. Through trauma, betrayal and wounds to near death, as well as self-destruction which culminated in the before mentioned collision of her pain and resistance with the most potent force in the Universe, she met the unending, unchanging love of the Good Shepherd. That combined with His patience and constant loving pursuit of His lamb gone astray. God the Father, the Creator, sent His Son, Jesus Christ, the Savior, for many reasons. We all need the redemption, the guidance, protection and loving care of our Creator. Jesus came to show us how we are loved by the Creator and the lengths He went to and continues to go to, keeping us close to Him, as a Good Shepherd does. (Col. 1:15,19)

Letter Two

My Beloved young Brave Heart,

What has happened to you? Little Brave Heart loved the Lord Jesus since she was five years old. She recognized His presence in her young life often and she knew He was her Savior. She was dedicated to Him from her mother's womb and was raised to know the truth about who He is and she trusted Him. What caused you to step away from His embrace and to resist His love? What motivated you to start running fast and hard from His presence and His voice?

Incest—a monstrous word; a monstrously horrid, reprehensible act--was inflicted on her more than once when she was seven or eight. It happened during a particularly stressful and tumultuous time. No one was paying attention and she was left alone with a male member of the extended family. This man chose to betray her with evil acts on three or four separate occasions during that season of distress. She was a prime target and her protectors were primarily distracted, therefore, the evil intentions were uninhibited. The molestation ended eventually, but it had opened the door and thus began the subsequent slow, continual rape of the soul. Robbed of innocence but left with a strong conviction that we must remain silent, we went underground with the horror. Soon, however, some of the effects of the sexual abuse began to surface and manifest. Outbursts and odd behaviors that were a direct result of the molestation began to show themselves but were ignored by anyone who might have been able to help her. Therefore, the cause of her root problem was left undiscovered and untreated and unresolved. Being abandoned emotionally by any and all protectors, who never followed up on their suspicions, she was forced to deal with the trauma and its consequences alone.

She was forever changed by the violation of her young body through incest. Knowledge of sexuality had not been part of her awareness as a child before the horrendous acts. It's difficult to explain all of the physical, mental and emotional effects that were initiated by and resulted from the molestation. Needless to say, it was devastating to the psyche and soul of our little Brave Heart.

As time passed and the incest remained a secret, the impact in her life was profound, young Brave Heart. Because of the emotional health of the family and support system, silence was modeled to her when it came to dealing with dirty, messy, shameful things. There was never any healthy confrontation of problems, let alone any healthy working toward resolution of problems. There was no safe place to turn to, no running to the arms of her protectors and no open communication that caused her to feel that she had a refuge. Therefore, she was forced to invent and emulate faulty coping mechanisms to keep the betrayal and her awakened sexuality hidden. At all costs. There were never any spoken rules, only her intuition that told her that silence was the law. As a result, she, an innocent child, was face to face with the reality of the robbery of her innocence. Her mind had been opened to her sexuality at age seven or eight, as had her body, but her emotional capacity to process it all fell far short. Having been robbed of the opportunity to enter adulthood according to the natural course of nature and godliness, she was forced in essence to react as a pseudo-adult. Confusion, of course, was her constant mental state. Somehow, at some point, a separation, a vacancy, took place in her soul, our soul, young Brave Heart. In order to cope, you, young Brave Heart, had to put the real little Brave Heart away—away somewhere that shame belonged. Her sexuality had been awakened and was alive and became a drive during puberty. You believed that she was damaged and shameful. So you put her where shame belonged. Underground. Little Brave Heart, the one who was innocent and had been violated somehow became the object of shame and abhorrence. You, young Brave Heart, took the object of shame and buried her alive—in a sewer hole in our soul, along with the violation and its effects unspoken and denied. Young Brave Heart, you placed her in the slimy pit of shame and took on her identity. You constructed out of cardboard a false, flimsy front and became an imposter, forming and maintaining a façade so that no one would suspect the horror that had been done and the horror that she might become. You became a manufactured, facsimile version of the actual little Brave Heart, a pretender, to keep up the appearance and to deny that the terrible betrayal had ever happened. You were the one who had buried her alive and kept her buried. You were the person who functioned in the world, masquerading as real little Brave Heart, determined to maintain the silent front, as per the unspoken, unwritten code in our family. Your loyalty to the family system, which was systemic and deep, became more important than dealing with, or even admitting to, the pain, confusion and isolation that you constantly lived in. The horrible place that you made in our soul was a pit--a deep, dark, slimy sewer hole that reeked of shame and betrayal. You covered it over and surrounded it with a wall of thorns so that no one could get near it or even suspect that it was there. Only shameful and disgusting things belonged there, out of sight.

With little Brave Heart now in the sewer hole and out of sight, the main goal of your young life became the maintenance and upkeep of the front, the façade. Sometime after going underground with the horror, the unacknowledged, unprocessed and untreated effects of the incest and the massive burden of keeping the secrets boiled over and out of the sewer hole where they were simmering and fermenting in a toxic brew. There were outbursts of anger bordering on rage that began to surface and manifest during puberty and your early teenage years. Of course, according to the insidious family code of silence, the adults in our life ignored these symptoms. Therefore, the root of these problems was left undiscovered by our protectors. Being abandoned emotionally by them only reinforced your view of being forced to deal with it all alone. Suppression was the only recourse open to you.

The violation of our body through incest changed us forever, young Brave Heart. It's difficult to explain and to understand all of the physical, mental and emotional rerouting that took place during and after the abuse. The foul, heinous acts stole so much from us, my Beloved. As you automatically progressed into puberty and the teenage years, the devastation to your psyche and soul were relieved only temporarily through acting with your peers and masturbation. Of course, this only added to the enormous load of guilt and shame and regret that you had to keep locked up in the sewer hole along with our real, little Brave Heart. The impact on your cardboard front and life as an imposter was profound. Lacking any healthy confrontation of your horror, let alone any healthy working toward resolution, you were left with no other choice but to continue on in the way of secrecy and duplicity. You were forced to invent and imitate self-destructive coping mechanisms to keep the betrayal, the incest and the abandonment hidden. At all costs. Continuing the masquerade, perpetuating the false front required all the strength that you could muster and over time it became second nature to you.

Determined as you were to maintain appearances and to remain silent, at some point you would need to employ another coping technique. Thus began the icing down and numbing of your emotions and sexual needs and responses. You convinced yourself that according to the family code of silence, the horror that had been done to little Brave Heart and the effects that you, the imposter, suffered silently didn't matter. They, along with you, weren't important. Your steely resolve was to continue to keep the trauma, the pain, and little Brave Heart in the sewer hole always, no matter the cost to yourself. At least the family system would continue to thrive, seemingly unscathed. Your thinking and reasoning continued to warp and become more and more toxic.

She, innocent little Brave Heart, could never reappear and disrupt the development of the cardboard life, the masquerade that you were carefully crafting. It would threaten the family system and reveal the tremendous viral machine it perpetuated. Not to mention the horrible forbidden fact that our sexuality had been awakened and discovered and been lethally tampered with. Consequently, you, cardboard, false young Brave Heart, must put away the sexual creature that you mistakenly believed little Brave Heart had become or would become if she were free from the sewer hole. This was the colossal lie that you lived with and kept hidden so well, young Brave Heart. The falsehood that you were the shameful thing that had happened to you. The real little Brave Heart could never be allowed to resurface. There was too much at stake and too much to lose if the truth ever came to light. The greatest tragedy is, of course, that your belief about her was greatly and tragically mistaken. Also, it was just as tragic that any emotionally healthy adult could have shattered that strong illusion if the truth had been brought to light and told.

It was during this time in your life, your teenage years, that you began morphing mentally and emotionally into plastic Brave Heart. The façade, the front, was becoming more solid over time. It was becoming fitted and less of an effort to uphold. It was seeking to become your identity, young Brave Heart. Your heart was hardening as well toward the Good Shepherd. You were never a better pretender than when you attended a church service or function. All the ingredients mixed together well in your determination to ignore and forget about Him. Surely we had become reprehensible to Him as well. Your campaign to conceal the truth from everyone included Him. So began the long season in our life of resistance to the Good Shepherd and His unending love for us. Clearly, the despicable thing that you were trying to avoid becoming couldn't go anywhere near where He was. In your child's mind you reasoned that you could control and deflect the Love of the Universe and hold Him at arm's length, along with everyone else. The childish reasoning and attempt to turn away from Him and His love only further strengthened and watered the hedge of thorns that was covering over the slimy pit where little Brave Heart lived in exile. What you didn't realize in your immaturity was of course that the love of the Good Shepherd would never be dissuaded and that He would never turn away in disgust or stop loving us no matter what happened or what we had done or thought about our self. The Lord of Life loved us eternally and truly. He would never cease to pursue us, wanting only to bring us back into His loving, everlasting arms. He had, all along, a safe place for us, made specifically for us, where He wanted to take us. A place where He could heal your wounds and change what you thought about little Brave Heart and Himself. He died for the shame you were trying above all else to keep concealed. You needed to understand that wholeheartedly and fully in order to be really free.

Living on as you did, unaware of this truth about the Good Shepherd, you—now plastic Brave Heart—had become the impression of little Brave Heart that you wanted the world to see. She had been violated and was now imprisoned deep in the putrid hole in our soul. What had happened to her, however, had not changed her. She had been the victim of a horrible sex crime, but it had not torn her identity to shreds as you believed it had. She remained the pure little Brave Heart because she belonged to the Good Shepherd first and foremost. She was wrongfully imprisoned and assumed to be guilty. She remained, however, the Brave Heart that she was born to be, unchanged and pure, no matter what had happened to her body. You, young Brave Heart, carried around the devastation that accompanies victimhood and the ravages of an innocent sexuality torn apart. These effects stayed with you; they were assumed by you even as you ignored the pain continually. The charges against little Brave Heart were false but you had believed her guilty, unfit, and you put her away. Thus, plastic Brave Heart grew and matured as a shadow of the true Brave Heart. What you believed her to be was what you actually lived out, secretly. You began and perfected a double life, presenting one face to the world and then living out secretly, what you thought she was—shameful, repulsive, unfit and undeserving of anything good. It was the perfect formula for self-hatred and ineffectiveness in life.

This was the beginning, Dear Reader, of the double life that formed outwardly and inwardly in order to function falsely as the real Brave Heart. It was a masquerade, a superb acting job, perfected to survive the horror that she thought she had successfully put away from herself and everyone else. She assumed the responsibility of protecting the very people who had betrayed her physically and abandoned her emotionally. No one would know the truth and plastic Brave Heart would master the evil power of keeping secrets and perfect the hazardous pretense of living a double life, aided by her ability to masterfully deceive herself and keep her emotions and desires iced down.

Little Brave Heart, the innocent one who was a double victim, was locked in a dark place that was covered over by a hedge of thorns to keep everyone away from discovering the truth. She would be a captive forever while plastic Brave Heart, who had assumed her identity, lived out her days as an imposter, a pretender with a secret, double life. All the while the sewer hole was being violently protected from discovery with all of the strength and power of deception that plastic Brave Heart could muster. The purpose was so that the family system, which was more important than any individual pain, could continue to function with all of its self righteousness and hypocrisy. Plastic Brave Heart remained true to the code of family loyalty and took upon herself the mantle of generational secrets and shame. At her young age, she began the false destiny of fully assuming the responsibility for maintaining the unspoken yet pervasive system of non-coping, non-disclosure and pretense that was strongly modeled to her from both sides of her family and support system. No one was going to get near the dark place in her soul and perhaps discover the kidnapping of little Brave Heart, who was being held captive unjustly. Plastic Brave Heart spent a tremendous amount of time and energy as a child, a teenager, and a young adult, perfecting the deception of the secret, double life. It was time that could have and should have been spent developing the personality, gifts, talents and destiny of little Brave Heart. Time also that could have been spent developing the relationship between Brave Heart and the lover of her soul, the Good Shepherd, Jesus Christ, the Son of God. She had trusted Him and loved Him. As a consequence of the trauma and its effects, she stepped away from His embrace and began to resist His love. She started running fast and hard from the security and peace of His presence and the assurance of His voice. Thus, the mantle of pain and wasted potential was being fitted and assumed by Brave Heart, thereby assuring the passing down of the painful, restrictive family system to the next generation.

Just know, Beloved Reader and young Brave Heart, that I see from my perspective in the Cleft, forty years from where you are now, that the moment you turned from Him and stiff armed His love, that He started reaching for you. The Good Shepherd left the flock, the other ninety-nine, and went seeking you, calling for you. He was relentless in His pursuit of you and He never ceased in His attempts to nudge you, lead you, love you back into the fold where you belonged and your true identity and destiny waited. As you begin to run and resist Him, as you were perfecting the false, double life, the unrecognized and untreated justifiable anger was lying undefined and festering in the sewer hole where you carefully placed it. It will lie undisturbed for many years. You are a master at keeping it hidden, all of it, as if it never existed at all. The buried anger however, is a living entity, brewing undisturbed, simmering into a thick toxic concoction. As it cooks there, unresolved and fermenting, it slowly marinates all of the contents of the sewer hole as it bubbles up into a silent but potent rage. Sudden outbursts of the putrid brew occasionally spill over and into your life despite your strength and consume you. The overwhelming nature of unprocessed, unresolved trauma that is left undiscovered, invalidated and unprocessed could be abated by the icing down process topped off with the consumption of gallons of alcohol. If there are any concerns about the occasional outwardly manifested anger, they are subsequently ignored and passed over. Consequently, the hideous, damaging residue of molestation and incest, pain, shame, guilt and inevitably, self-loathing all remain shoved down, buried alive in that secret, slimy compartment. Left to itself, it only continues to boil and brew into a recipe of poison, ripe with self-hatred and potential self-destruction. Sometime the stench of the foul brew boiling down in the hole becomes too much to bear and keep hidden. No one must ever know or even suspect the truth. To assist you in the endeavor of falsehood is the system—ironclad and binding. It is the subculture of denial and unresolved pain that is lubricated and kept operational by the idle worship of family loyalty. The system shows you how to function in spite of the damaging pain, the screaming pain that must remain muted. You must act like it doesn't really matter. Even better, lie to yourself and pretend that it never happened. It's not important; subsequently, you are not important. What really counts is maintaining the façade of goodness, never showing how desperately needy and bereft we are. The kicker, Brave Heart, is the self-reliant, self-righteous, prideful and evil-serving system of survival that is quickly morphing you into a different person, far from your true self, the innocent victim. The lack of authenticity in your soul, plastic Brave Heart, serves only to lock you into a cocoon, isolated and stunted.

The inability to deal honestly with your real life issues rises to the surface as you develop physically and physiologically as a teenager. Your sexually-awakened body, one result of the molestation, is suddenly on fire with desire.

The only choice, the only way to stave off the waves of physical craving, is to act out. It must be done in secret as well, of course. The dilemma is, however, that the fire is never completely quenched. Your body eventually aches for more, an unfortunate and inappropriate state for an eleven or twelve year old to endure. In a mixture of revulsion, confusion, you seek relief for the torture. Putting little Brave Heart away hasn't stopped it or slowed it down. Stopping short of intercourse, the only recourse is experimentation with your peers and the virtual prison of masturbation. The added shame that this creates in your already guilt-ridden psyche causes you to take the drastic step of putting away the real part of us, young Brave Heart. Along with little Brave Heart, you bury our normal, healthy sexual development. You have already begun the masterful pretense that has become the silent center and driving force of your plastic life. Any sense of self-respect and healthy self-love is buried with her along with any chance of healthy development of our God-given sexuality. After burying her, you begin the process of icing down your emotions and your sex drive so that you can impersonate little Brave Heart flawlessly.

In the absence of healthy self-love and self-respect, the picture of who you are that you carry with you is warped. Because of the unresolved trauma, plastic Brave Heart, your substitute soul is slowly being put to death. The subculture of pain, modeled to you by your family systems,

is fueled by silence and lack of conflict resolution result-
ing in layer upon layer of untreated, unexposed issues and
malfunction. With all of your strength you keep trying
to hold back the avalanche of accumulated and inherited
pain but eventually the boiling putrid brew in your soul
overflows in the form of self-destructive thoughts, behaviors and actions. The monumental task of upholding
the falsehoods, the manufactured life, the plastic person,
the effects of victimization and the imprisonment of little
Brave Heart. The only hint of pain that escapes unguard-
ed comes in the form of the learned and developed weap-
on of sarcasm. It also runs through and is fueled by the
subculture of pain and denial. It is an effective deflecting
skill that works well as a guardian of the sewer hole. Sarcasm reveals the thorniness in your soul but is sufficient
enough to keep anyone away from the source of the pain.

During our childhood and teenage years young, plastic
Brave Heart, you come close to perfecting the insidious
pretense, almost mastering the job of keeping the effects
of our stolen childhood and the loss of our precious innocence covered according to the rules and operation of the
subculture of denial, which in turn maintains the upkeep
of the mountainous iceberg of family loyalty above all else.
Anything right or true about our self concept or sexuality
is mashed together and mixed into the putrid brew in the
dark hold where true little Brave Heart remains a prison-
er. You continue to function outwardly according to the

code but all the while this lethal combination is rising to the top of the sewer hole and gaining control, becoming your normal. It's attempting to settle in as your identity. You become more distant, detached emotionally and remote inwardly. In maintaining the plastic façade according to the unwritten code of the unspoken subculture, you grow further away from any true and honest relationships with others and you also withdraw farther from the Good Shepherd, whom you once loved.

You can't fight it. You don't know that you need to fight it young Brave Heart. I can see it from here, precious one, from my view in the Cleft. You have disposed of little Brave Heart, assumed her identity and now you are headlong in the development of the false, double life that was never intended for her, for us. It's so bizarre and twisted, but I can see that as a child and a teenager you don't have the awareness or the strength to swim out of the murky waters, the layers of the generational subculture of pain. Lacking an intervention and any treatment or resolution of the effects of the titanic, monstrous betrayal and abandonment, you are rendered emotionally stunted, isolated and cut off. In your effort to adapt and compensate, you have created and developed an altered image of the real little Brave Heart, the victim, who is locked away unjustly. Young Brave Heart has skillfully created a false persona, who is skilled at adapting and functioning. Bound and determined to keep the turmoil of the truth and all of its unknown repercussions closed off to the light of day and any semblance of true life and love is by far the greatest mode of self-hatred and a slow and effective form of self destruction. The true and wonderful life that the Good Shepherd had in store for little Brave Heart all along is in serious danger of being forever wasted and lost. She had accepted Him as that true life and true love, ensuring forever that she would belong to, even as she was imprisoned in the sewer hole illegally and unfairly by you, young Brave Heart. It was your choice to bury her there and to leave her there, but as a child victim of a sex crime, you were not being held responsible. Our protectors should have somehow discovered the truth and intervened, initiating a process of recovery and healing. The subculture of denial and pain should have been denied the power over your life and your choices. As a child, you should have never been left to your own ends, to manufacture your own way. They were so conditioned by the subculture themselves, our protectors, that they chose to ignore and not see or act on the signs, the indications that a powerful change had taken place in us during early childhood. They did see at one point that we had become a changed child, different from the precious little Brave Heart that they had known. They fell short, abandoning us emotionally. What choice was left? The responsibility of assuming and carrying on with the mantle of emotional sickness fell hard and heavy on your shoulders. Someday you would be obligated, according to the code, to drape the same heavy mantle of inherited, horrendous dysfunction on your own child's shoulders, thereby perpetuating the evil, lying system onto another generation of innocents. There didn't seem to be a choice for us then. Our job was to protect the glacier of lies, secrets and emotional sickness as it slid its way down through the generations, leaving untold amounts of rocky soil in the souls of the families that it overtook and flattened in its wake. Its job was to nullify and render ineffective the Creator's plan for greatness in each life year after year.

In the midst of your manufactured flow however, in spite of the noise of the glacier of ice careening its way down through the generations, leaving them impotent and stealing destinies, there remained a still, small, peaceful voice, cutting through the stubborn attitude of your justifiable anger. There was an occasional nudge, all along the way, of the Good Shepherd's staff, gentle but noticeable. Could it be Him, the real, true love of your life.... Yes, He is calling us Brave Heart, as a child, as a teenager, as a young adult. I can see it clearly from here, in the Cleft. He is seeking us, loving us. He is gently trying to bring us back into His embrace, into the safety of His arms. You have been running from that embrace since the victimization and the banishment of little Brave Heart to the sewer hole of shame. I see you at the age of twelve, responding to Him and making a public profession of your faith in

Him. You even testify about Him in front of a group of people in church. For a short time then, you remember the brightness of His love and the freedom and security that you once enjoyed in His love, before the despicable betrayal of our childhood and the imprisonment of the innocent little girl. Is there enough power there though to overturn the subculture of pain and its grip on us? Is there enough grace to render it null and void? The twisting in your soul and the truth of His love seem to run parallel in your life. Is there an intersection somewhere? The shame and unworthiness combined with the self loathing that has permeated the soul of you, manufactured, plastic Brave Heart, seems to speak more loudly than His voice of freedom. The grip of the subculture of pain and denial only grows stronger and the mantle of pride that it provides only grows heavier as you grow older. You have learned to bow to the idol of family loyalty and secrecy on a daily basis. The self-righteousness of the system has you clasped tightly in its grasp. The wall protecting it is made of secret pain and has you hemmed in on every side. It seems impenetrable to you. It is screaming at you, closing in—you will never leave us, it whispers wickedly. And yet....

Letter Three

Dearest Brave Heart,

I see you in the fall of our eighteenth year. By now, the subculture of pride, pain and denial is ingrained and firmly fixed in your self-concept. It is always there, constraining, binding and hindering your thought processes and your actions. It is second nature to you by now to function as a pretender. You seem to have mastered the pretense of disguising yourself as the real, innocent but imprisoned little Brave Heart. The unwritten rules of the code of pretension, self-righteousness and silence, the force that binds it all together into a lethal machine that by now operates almost automatically and without question. Never questioned by you or any others who have passed it down and keep it enforced with a stubborn resolve. There lies within you, in the deepest part of you, a dissatisfaction, a stirring, a longing, an almost completely muted sense of destiny. It remains unrecognized and indefinable but it succeeds in sparking a small sense of unrest. Not the same unrest caused by the mountain of unresolved issues in your life; in fact, the two sparks of unrest are opposed to each other. I can hear it from here, young Brave Heart, from within the Cleft. It's the voice of little Brave Heart, calling out for freedom, for release from the scum hole! You are more familiar with pain and pretense than the sound of her voice, and you misinterpret the sound of her cries. It sounds vaguely like a call of destiny, a deep strong desire for something more. That's impossible though, you reason. Because of what has happened, what you have done, Brave Heart has been disqualified from any destiny and must settle for less, for whatever you can find. So, you continue on, intent on drowning out the deep desire for more, doing whatever it takes to avoid the gentle nudge of the Good Shepherd's staff. An expert at running straight away from the truth, you take a turn in the opposite direction, away from freedom, health and life. Fear of exposure, terrified that someone will hack through the hedge of thorns in your soul and discover the sewer hole, you flee almost full force from any inkling of the goodness and deliverance that is available to you any time. The belief that you are what you think she is—full of shame and deserving what has been done to her—dogs your trail every day. The longer the betrayal remains untreated and unresolved, the more twisted it is becoming in your soul. Your true identity is in danger of remaining in the slime hole forever, or so you believe. I can see it from here, in the Cleft, the safe place to heal, many years down the road from where you are my precious one.

Finally, a chance for perhaps a new beginning comes in the fall of that year as you enter college. Removed physically from subculture of pain and denial brings some temporary mental relief but before long you will enter into a long season of yet more turmoil and fear which will activate a new level of avoidance, suppression and compounded pressure that will test the limits of the system and your resolve to maintain the pretense. The price of maintaining the secret sewer hole in your soul is about to come due young Brave Heart.

In January of 1979, you notice a black mole on your left shoulder that had not been there before. It is biopsied and diagnosed and on March 1 you receive a phone call in your dorm room on campus. It's malignant. A melanoma in stage three of four stages. The news drops on you like a huge boulder. The stress and confusion compounds your already tangled emotional health. The reality of the word cancer brings a ringing death sentence to your pretenders' coping skill set. This is something that can't be avoided or run from. This gaping and yawning hole of the unknown sparks a dramatic increase in the intensity of your spinning away from the real source of comfort and help, the Good Shepherd. The startling emotional effects of course, bounce off of your psyche that has been trained and conditioned to deny the truth of how you are going to deal with this. What you have given the most energy to during your life since the betrayal and incest—anger, not coping, not processing, just surviving and self-destruction—are now on the front burner with the potential to be manifested exponentially.

After undergoing surgery, which was the only choice when dealing with melanoma in 1979, the façade remains intact. Plastic Brave Heart steps up to the plate and hits a grand slam in maintaining the front, the appearance. All the while though, you are limping emotionally and mentally, very much closed off to the Good Shepherd, whom you are holding at arm's length, in spite of the many prayers of many faithful that love you. From my perspective here in the Cleft, I see the grace and mercy that lifted you and covered you during that time young Brave Heart. Someday you will see it also.

Deflecting the fear with humor, you deal with this extremely traumatic event with a stern, stoic resolve mixed with some sarcastic comic relief to break the tension for everyone else. The best defense against the landslide of fear is the 'iceberg effect'. You know it so well, Brave Heart. Just stay in character, take it in stride to protect everyone else. In your numb state and your youth, the full ramifications of the situation escape you anyway. Remain in the iced down buffer zone. It's in full force. It never enters your mind to bring it all down to the bare bones to process it all emotionally and mentally, as per the code. If the emotional dam is ever broken, if the sewer hole is discovered, there is a danger that the whole behemoth of your pretense may come to light and that would be worse than eventually succumbing to any recurring malignancy. If the code is broken and the family system is smashed open and destroyed, how will we live? If the mantle of secret pain is shed by you, how will the subculture fostered by many generations function? It's up to you young Brave Heart, or so you believe, to maintain the glacier, the mountain of pride and self-righteousness no matter the cost to you. Therefore, you believe that you have no choice and you continue on in the groove of staunch, self-control. There is no reaching you, bound and determined to plow the rocky field of your life alone with a three-legged mule. Go on, young Brave Heart, bounce off every nasty rock in every row of that field. Resist every godly attempt at reconciliation with the Good Shepherd. Leave little Brave Heart in the scum hole, crying out for freedom. Anger brewing into rage is the driving force in your life now—it's entrenched in you. The combination of childhood sexual trauma and a cancer diagnosis as a teenager has you wrapped up so tightly that you can't begin to unwind it. Giving up would mean upsetting the functioning dysfunction of your life and your belief system, as well as that of the patriarch, matriarch and perpetrator of the molestation. The whole extended family system would blow up and be destroyed. Or so you believe. They and you wouldn't know how to live if the truth were known or told. Or so you believe. What has happened to you and how you have reacted to it has disqualified you from any good plan that the Good Shepherd might have had in mind for you. From this point on, just remain numb, iced down. This is the strongest coping skill when mixed with denial. This is how you keep walking and bouncing and spinning through the next three or four years, young Brave Heart. It's the only way to keep up the pretense. Living habitually in an unauthentic manner is the only way you know how to live. Unfortunately, however, this kind of living can only spiral downward. You are becoming more lost, Brave Heart, and the despondency is showing despite the masquerade. I can see it from here.

Thankfully, during this monstrously difficult time, there are several caring others who trust the Good Shepherd, the Lord of glory, for you, Brave Heart. Their faith, combined with one gift of faith in particular, is what will bring you through this stormy season, at least in a physical sense. You're still alive. There are one or two sincere attempts made by some who love the Good Shepherd to lead you to emotional recovery after your surgery. Nothing really grasps you and powers your swim out of the pit of your pain. You're too angry and scared. Many seeds are planted in the hard, rocky ground of your soul. Now they need to be watered.

Looking back as I am at that time in your life here in the Cleft, I gained the understanding many years later that in actuality the truth is that the cancer, the melanoma, was a symptom in your troubled life. It was as if the malignancy was an outbreak of the poison in your soul, an almost inevitable result stemming from covering and holding down the rage, pain and shame that was fertilized by the putridness locked up in the sewer hole. It couldn't be contained any longer. What was buried alive in you had seeped out and had rooted and sprouted up into the acidity of cancer, watered and well cared for by the system of silence. Secrets buried alive remain alive and thrive in the unresolved and unprocessed ground of denial and suppression. That black mole on your shoulder was the sign of the sickness in your soul coming to light at last.

What had been planted in you, betrayal, molestation, robbery of your innocence, premature sexuality, deception, self-hatred and many more insidious results of living a false, manufactured life had turned you to stone, Brave Heart. Much work lies ahead for the sculptor, our Michelangelo, the Helper. Real little Brave Heart lies buried deep in the marble of our false life plastic Brave Heart. It going to take a skilled, loving hand to reveal her again and then only if the marble itself will allow the chipping away to take place.

None of this was the fault of little Brave Heart. She was betrayed and molested and determined to be shameful, so she was put away, buried. What we failed to understand, though, is that she belonged to the Good Shepherd and always remained wrongfully imprisoned. He, the Lord of Life, maintained her while she was in the despicable hole. She would never become what had been done to her in spite of what you thought young Brave Heart. You had put her in that horrendous place because of the false beliefs perpetuated by the destructive subculture of your family system. Therefore, I was the one who had to release her. Through the process of recovery many years after the tragic abuse, I learned the truth. The truth about her, the imposter that you became after putting her in the hole. Most importantly, I learned the truth about who she was, where she was and the truth about her innocence, which is unchangeable, no matter the circumstances of your life, where you go or what you do.

From the perspective of the Cleft, on the shores of recovery and restoration where I now live, it is safe to say that the scummy sewer hole and the energy that it takes to keep it covered doesn't stand to remain intact and in control of your life, young Brave Heart. Its power to drive you and motivate you to a subpar life and eventual self-destruction won't last long in light of the love and power of the restorative grace of the Good Shepherd. Once the power of it is given completely into the hands of the Lord of Love, the progressive healing process will begin. He will never force you into anything, young Brave Heart, but His goodness and mercy will guide you into this freedom. Don't resist for much longer—you are twenty-two years old. Your life is waiting for you.

Letter Four

My dear young Brave Heart,

I love you. It's one of the most important things that I have learned to do while I have been in the Cleft. I have learned how to be honest. Assuming the victimhood status of little Brave Heart, you became a world-class liar. Dishonesty that you told yourself was necessary. You were conditioned and fooled into believing that the maintenance of the family system was honorable and vital. That meant that putting away little Brave Heart was necessary and vital. The code could never be broken by you telling the truth about the betrayal and molestation of little Brave Heart by a male member of your extended family. This is what you believed and what was modeled and reinforced to you over and over in our childhood. This wrong thinking justified the double, plastic life that you fabricated when you took her place in the world. It also fueled what you believed about her, that she was repulsive, unfit and undeserving of anything good, which is the perfect formula for self-hatred and ineffectiveness in life. You tried to use it to cope, to survive what had happened to her and to survive the horror as a pretender. You truly convinced yourself that no one would ever know the truth and that you could master the evil power of keeping secrets and perfect the hazardous pretense of living a double life.

Little Brave Heart was locked in a dark place, destined to be a captive forever while you lived out her days as an imposter, a liar. You violently protected the sewer hole from discovery, with all the strength and power of deception that you could muster. All of this was for the sake of the family system, so that it could continue to function, locked up with falsehood and hypocrisy. Plastic Brave Heart, you remained true to the code of family loyalty and took upon yourself the mantle of generational secrets and shame. At your young age you began the process of fully assuming the responsibility in order to be able to pass it down to the next generation.

During the ages of eighteen through twenty-two, the difficult fight for you comes not in a physical sense. No sign of the malignancy ever shows itself again, even after a second surgery on another suspicious mole on your back in 1981. The mental and emotional strain increases, however, because of the medical prognosis. Tremendously and miraculously, because of the goodness, mercy and faithfulness of the Good Shepherd, the Redeemer, the prayers of many believers and Christ followers were positively answered. The original biopsy contained all of the cancer in your body. The ominous blackness manifesting itself in your body was reduced to one dark speck. The truth and reality of this miracle is somehow overshadowed by the doctor's prediction of a probable recurrence that would lead to your death within three to five years. It must be hiding somewhere in your body, they said, waiting for your blood to carry it to other areas and organs. Thus began the real battle for your life. Would the cancer someday return and end your life or would you take it upon yourself to do the deed?

It is the emotional and mental stress of the combination of traumas that takes their toll on you young Brave Heart. The continuing, persistent, and unprocessed pain accumulates and thrives. The heavy mantle of loyalty to family pride and secrets, fitted for you to wear and then pass to the next generation of innocents, has become the most important part of your wardrobe since the betrayal and incest in your childhood when you assumed the identity of little Brave Heart. You are unable to take responsibility for yourself, plastic Brave Heart, stumbling and fumbling around with no real direction or purpose or goals. How can you? As a pretender, you have no real identity or legs to stand on as a young adult. Once, long ago, you loved the Good Shepherd. You trusted Him and entered His arms and became a part of His flock eternally. His love will never leave little Brave Heart, who was locked in the slimy pit of shame surrounded by thorns. In stubborn desperation, you continue to keep Him at arm's length, consumed by the pain and anger. In order to survive and to merely pass through young adulthood, you work continuously to keep your heart, emotions and sexuality iced down so that you will have plenty of strength to keep the lid clamped down tight on the sewer hole and the hellish brew fermenting there. Keeping little Brave Heart hidden is your primary goal. There is no energy or motivation left to find a place to grow or thrive. All you can do is pass the time, whatever time you have left that is.

The lack of knowledge of who the Good Shepherd really is and who little Brave Heart really is leads you in all of your plastic, manufactured falsehood down a path that only the lack of identity and the twistedness of false reality can. You fail in school, you fail at becoming gainfully employed, you fail at having any real plans for the future. You are floundering, young Brave Heart, badly. You are constructing an annex to the well of shame in your soul, to contain what you will add to it over the course of your plastic lifetime. But there is a striking difference in its foundation. There are cracks in the mortar of its foundation from the pressure and strain. Little Brave Heart continues her calling for freedom from within the sewer hole and many loving believers and Christ followers continue with their faith filled prayers for you. The scummy sewer hole was dug out and founded on the shifting sand of lies, wrong belief, unbelief and deception. There is no structural integrity that can withstand the faith filled, fervent prayers of the righteous. The gentle nudging and drawing of the Good Shepherd only grows stronger as you continue to resist His love, in answer to the prayers of the faithful. In spite of the culture of pain, there is a sense of sweetness and security beckoning you, inviting you to shed the heavy mantle of family loyalty and dysfunction. Out of habit and fear of the unknown and driven by a sense of unworthiness and self-loathing, you keep pushing back against the loving nudges. It is not for you. It can't be for you because of what you have done. Your impersonation of little Brave Heart and your attempt to live out what you falsely believe she deserves, a sub-par life, is what you stubbornly think you need to maintain. What has been done to her, and what you have done also, has disqualified her and you from a life of goodness and any destiny that was planned by the Good Shepherd. Any sense of a purposeful, productive life lived for Him must be forgotten. You believe that she doesn't deserve freedom and a peaceful, productive life. What's left, you reason, is the substitute life that you have been manufacturing since you banished little Brave Heart, the golden part of us, the potential in us to grow into His image, to the scummy sewer hole. The self-loathing is very pervasive, Brave Heart, and it has and will affect important choices that you have made and may make in the future. It is the most dangerous and inhibitive device that you have assimilated from the subculture of pain. It's who you think she is, we are, damaged and shameful and bound to live a sub par life. The evil that was done has almost succeeded in making you believe that it is our destiny. That our life will never rise above what has been done. We must settle for less, waste our potential, to maintain the front. The only response to this conclusion, this identity saturated with self-hatred is of course, self-destruction. There are many forms from which to choose. Some are slower and some would be more direct. One will drag out the hidden, double life and another, a more drastic measure, will end it all...the pain and the pretense, the futility of ever hoping or attaining anything more than what you see today.

Amazingly though, my precious one—and I can see it clearly from here—in the midst of your pain and confusion, in all those years spent running, there is a whisper, a drawing, a kind word from someone speaking His name to you. All of this has not been totally drowned out by your stubborn avoidance and pride. The Good Shepherd has not left His search for you, Brave Heart, He has not forgotten or left you alone. The voice of little Brave Heart continues to cry out to Him from inside the slimy pit of shame that you tried to hide her in. She still belongs to Him and is innocent, with her destiny still intact. It has never been revoked or altered because of the betrayal or

your impersonation of her. The Good Shepherd is longing to restore her to you, to us. His life is within her and
all of His potential and plans for us lie within her as well.

Meanwhile, while little Brave Heart and the Good
Shepherd wait, you are determined still to hold Him at
arm's length. The diagnosis of the cancer and the prognosis of eventual early death, combined with the betrayal
and its effects, have you frozen, numb and paralyzed. You
have never truly grappled honestly with any of the past or
the prospects of the future. The passionate fear and dread
of pain, suffering and death ring in your soul and hang in
your consciousness continuously. It's insidious and there
is no cure, physically or emotionally. There is only a short
future, or so you believe. Eventually, the cancer will me-
tastasize and reappear, probably before you are twenty-
five. More than likely it will end in agonizing death. Your
body has been cut and left deformed in the hope of saving
you for only a short time. It's excruciating. It's beyond
your ability to cope with or process. So you continue the
pattern of resistance, numbly running, mostly in circles.

During one cold January night in 1981, the battle for
your life is raging. This may be the time—the fight, the
numbness, the resistance, and the pain has exhausted you,
Brave Heart. Your resolve to hold the pretense together
no matter the cost to yourself has worn down almost to a
thread. Until now, poisoning yourself with alcohol continuously and on numerous occasions has only worked as

a tool to maintain the numbness and to avoid the truth. It has not succeeded in killing you. You can actually hear an echo in your mind of a voice telling you to end it all now. So you run. You climb out of a basement window and head out on foot in the dark. You run in the direction of a favorite park, a place you used to walk with your dog. During your teenage years you found some peace there, actually lying in the grass on a hillside, thinking about your Savior momentarily. That night, however, as you run, the voice is following, screaming very loudly. End it! When you cross the small creek, you approach a shelter house. Surprisingly, a length of rope is tied to the upper part of one of the support posts. *Here it is!* the voice screams. *Try it on for size. It fits*—Brave Heart, for a moment you are in agreement with the evil one, the enemy of your soul. The pain, the rage, the secrets would die with you. It will be your final act in maintaining the covenant of secrecy. As you place the looped rope around your neck, you hear the voice of the Good Shepherd, the voice of peace. Not a nudge, not a draw. He speaks to your mind, to your heart. "Take it off. Don't do it. You will never know how things will turn out if you do this." The strong, sure voice of peace breaks the power of the attempt on your life, Brave Heart. The gentleness of His touch brings a spark of hope that had been missing. Hope for a future. Ending it all by your own hand would have made you guilty of grand larceny. Robbing you of your future, robbing your family and friends who would never understand and robbing the Good Shepherd of His destiny for you. The power of His death and resurrection purchased a bright and hopeful future for us, Brave Heart, as it has for everyone who belongs to Him. Hang onto that gentle voice and the promise of a future, a destiny. You are far away from Him and that destiny but He is very near to you, waiting for you to turn and make one step toward Him, into His open arms.

As you leave the rope hanging, you run on. Eventually, you return home that night safely. But as you continue running in the months ahead, the thought of suicide never again enters your mind. Perhaps there is a crack in the mortar of the sewer hole after all. The dark hole remains in place for many months after this point in time but- you responded to the voice of the Good Shepherd, Brave Heart. There is a tiny seed of trust in your heart. Hope is coming, but He will continue to nurture the seed of trust that is being watered by the prayers of the believers and Christ followers who love you, precious one.

During the course of the next two years, as you continue to resist Him and fullness of His love, you travel and seek to find a place where you can find contentment in spite of Him and His goodness. Everywhere you go is a dead end as you continue to carry on in the form of the mantle bearer of the subculture of pain, secretly upholding and protecting the family system at the expense of little Brave Heart's life. The stubborn system has an iron grip on you and it always strangles contentment and satisfaction with life. Everywhere and anywhere you go, it never fails when you arrive there, you find that the Good Shepherd is already there, patiently waiting, wanting you. And yet you still limp on, resisting Him.

By the end of 1982, you are nearing the end of your list of places to go to and try to find something...anything. You are running out of ways to avoid the nudging of the Good Shepherd, which has never ceased. You have been living a paradox since the night of the battle with suicide. You keep searching for ways and for a place where the manufactured life can thrive. In the meantime, an idea keeps building in you, an echo of something that you might have always known. Something that the Lord has always had in mind for Brave Heart, little Brave Heart. He wants you to be a missionary.

The circumstances in your manufactured, plastic life are narrowing Brave Heart. The power of the paradox is intensifying. The gentle voice of the Good Shepherd is whispering to your heart. The nudging of His shepherd's staff is directing you. Brave Heart, you have run almost to the end of your plastic self. His love is softening your hardened, broken Heart. Very soon this love and the destructive forces wanting your life are going to meet head on. The way of pain and secrecy that you have followed and believed, the entrapment you have languished in has been counterfeit. It was never meant for us, but you don't know how to turn around and you don't have the power to. That is why you have been bouncing and spinning, at a greater rate since the cancer diagnosis. As you choose to pay attention to and to listen to the gentle voice of the Good Shepherd, the knowing in your soul gets stronger. Even as you continue to hurt and suffocate and drown in the layers of pain that you have become so accustomed to. You believe that is what you must do, as the maintainer and mantle bearer of the family system of secret, unresolved pain. The old, putrid subculture fights hard to maintain its grip on you—and us—little Brave Heart must remain hidden so that the dysfunction becomes your identity, destiny and most importantly, your legacy. This is how the evil glacier continues to slide down inadvertently through the generations.

Then, suddenly, early in 1983, you are beginning to make seemingly ridiculous plans to follow the Good Shepherd on an overseas trip with a missionary organization. The gentle nudging has never ceased and in all of your running and spinning and seeking, you have found nothing else to sink yourself into. Everything else you've tried has come to a dead end. No place to live, no job or school seems to fit or feel right. Somehow you understand that He is leading you on this undertaking. You are sure of nothing else. You choose the missionary organization at random and begin the application process. There are references required in order to be accepted for the trip to Asia. For some reason, you choose the man who is the strangest Christian that you know. He is your father's best friend and he is one that has been regularly and fervently praying for you. He is the one who interceded in prayer for you the night before the melanoma surgery almost four years before. He is the one who groaned in intercession for you. (See Romans 8:26.) He is also the one who was in the waiting room with your parents during the operation and was there when the report came that you were cancer free. This same man invited you to his home one evening to discuss your upcoming trip. It was March 1, 1983, four years to the day that you had received the cancer diagnosis over the phone in your dorm room at college. The evil system that thrived on secrecy and hidden, unprocessed pain is about to be met head on—with the truth!

In his home that evening, our dad's best friend, the man who had been praying for you as if you were his own child, proceeded to tell you about the intercessory prayer time four years before, the night before the first surgery. The gift of faith became a real miracle and translated into a complete physical healing for us, Brave Heart. (I Cor 12:9) The assurance of this tremendous grace came to this friend during the prayer time and the reality of it showed true the next day when there was no cancer to be found in your shoulder, neck or jaw. There was a great concern that a lump found in your neck during a pre-op exam was indicative of the spread of the malignancy from the original site on your shoulder to perhaps your neck and head. When the black mole taken from your shoulder was biopsied, it was in the third of four stages of development. The healing miracle was complete and final, however. There were no more traces of cancer in your body and there would never be again.

As he tells you this account, face-to-face, in the front room of his house, the whole rest of the world seems to fall away, as do the scales on your eyes, heart and mind. You really hear the truth, seemingly for the first time. The room seems to be filled to the brim—full of the presence of the Good Shepherd and His manifest presence, the Helper, the Comforter. The Prince of Peace came to rule where before there had been fear, unbelief and hard-hearted, stubborn resistance fueled by your entrenched rage. That night, Brave Heart, your manufactured, pretending self fell in love with the King of Kings, Jesus Christ. Your drive to run and resist changed instantly to a heartfelt desire to yield to Him, to follow Him and to come to know Him intimately. You left that meeting forever changed and on a different path, Brave Heart. As you accepted the truth about the miracle of physical healing that took place in your body, the power of the revelation opened your eyes and your understanding. The redeeming love of the Healer released you from a multitude of misunderstanding about Him and yourself. You knew that the effectual, fervent prayers of righteous people had come into agreement with the will of the Father, and that you had been delivered, now and forever. The fear of dying has been blasted away. The door to healing the devastation in your soul has been opened to the power of the finished redemptive work of Christ and the ministry of the Helper. You most definitely experienced the mighty rushing wind of the Spirit of health and life in that living room that night. Love and mercy and relief surrounded you and became actual possessions of yours. You came home to the Good Shepherd that night, Brave Heart, and our life was set upon a continuing, progressive path of healing that would lead you eventually here, to the Cleft. It will be a thirty-plus-year journey of walking with your Jesus, the Good Shepherd, from there to here, beloved Brave Heart. What began that night in that front room is the beginning of your real life. The Good Shepherd is picking up from where you were derailed in your relationship with Him, from the time that little Brave Heart loved Him, before she was betrayed and molested and abandoned emotionally as a young child.

The path from that night of healing in March of 1983, until you reach the Cleft in 2004, is where you will find your life, your life in Christ. The life that He had intended for you, for us. Moving forward, with your hand in His, He will be formed in you. There is so much inward work to be done before your eventual reunion with little Brave Heart. Let our Michelangelo, the Helper, do His sculpting work. You will make mistakes but now you are walking toward a destination instead of in circles, limping. Your soul will heal. You have so much to look forward to, my beloved Brave Heart. I can't wait for your arrival here in the Cleft.

The process of recovery that began that night in 1983 in your young adulthood will blossom and become a journey into discipleship, love and eventually, bond-slavery to the Good Shepherd. Since the night of your 360 degree turn, you have fallen so deeply in love with the most infinitely awesome person in the universe, Jesus Christ, the Son of God. As you grow into your life in Christ, the work in your soul will continue progressively as you walk in step with Him. A life of peace and direction, preserved, held and renewed. Keep coming—with your hand in His. I can't wait for you to get here.

Letter Five

My dear precious Brave Heart,

As you carry on with the Good Shepherd and the Helper, the presence of the Lord in the Earth and everywhere, trust His grace to keep you. Through the course of time, many of the deeper issues that had a lock on you will be brought to the surface and lovingly dealt with. These issues separated you from little Brave Heart and shredded your manufactured soul, and are buried under the layers that are covering the sewer hole of shame where she remains, crying out. You are committed to Christ the Good Shepherd now and He is committed to you and always has been. Even so, you are still living as a pretender. The double life that you adapted and formed to survive the banishment and separation from little Brave Heart is still strong and pervasive. The power of the human will to maintain the secret subculture is remarkably stubborn and unwilling to disengage. The freedom to live as a changed, honest disciple is not welcomed in your family of origin. No one wants you to be depressed or despondent, but no one wants you to be completely honest and free either. The participants in the subculture of pain, denial and family loyalty based in self-righteousness, continue on in the same way, never confronting or acknowledging the truth about the hidden evil that is being passed down and assumed by each new generation of innocents.

After the life-altering night in March of 1983, you finally have enough conviction and strength from the Helper to admit the truth about the evil violation of little Brave Heart when she was very young. You forgive the betrayal and molestation and the admission of it is finally given to the matriarch of the maintenance of the subculture. She admonishes you to never tell the patriarch of your pain. Even though she confesses that she knew "something' was wrong" and after a certain point in your childhood that you "just weren't the same little girl anymore," she is afraid of how our dad will react and therefore we should do nothing. There is no astonishment, no horror, no chagrin, no sympathy. This response only further reinforces the premise of the subculture of silence. Consequently, at the age of twenty-three, it is further confirmed and reinforced to you Brave Heart that we live under a 'no-tell policy' in this family. We must soldier on, living out the iron clad rule of 'we don't tell and we pretend that it doesn't really matter even if it did happen'. And so, the deadly game of pretense continued for you young Brave Heart. Telling the truth and gaining any resolution of the pain was out of the question. Little Brave Heart, the victim of the betrayal and molestation must remain locked in the sewer hole, full of the muck of shame and aged anger. She must never reappear, be restored or reveal the truth. Maintaining the family system was far more important. So, in our young adulthood, even after renewing your relationship with the Good Shepherd, you still fitted yourself with the heavy, weighted mantle of familial loyalty. You must bear it and wear it, no matter the cost to yourself. That was the lesson learned—over and over and over—you must make a bed for yours and their dysfunction and nurse the emotional illness the rest of your days, passing it along to your innocent ones one day. You belonged to them by blood and biology—but you belonged to the Good Shepherd by spirit and truth. His redemptive work on the cross and His resurrection changed the rules and they belonged to you. He had purchased a better life for you and your innocence Brave Heart. He was leading you there, to that better life, slowly but surely. You belonged to Him and He would not leave you there. Keep following Him, keep in step with Him and hold His hand, all the way here to the Cleft. He will take you through a holy process here. Allow Him to fit you inside the safe place so that you can heal, really heal. It will change your life forever, the life of your innocence and the legacy you will leave for your grandchildren.

Until you reach the Cleft, the Good Shepherd will continue His work in your heart and soul. He will skillfully chip away the hardness of the human condition as you make your way to where I am because you ask Him to. Instinctively, you know that there is deep pain to be resolved and you also know that there is a deep healing waiting to be obtained and assimilated into your life. The Good Shepherd never pushes you; He only gently leads as He did before. Yet, you know that there is no turning back. The insidious code continues to cause pain and bind you. It will take time for more awareness and understanding to come, along with a desire for the deep things to change. As time passes and you remain in a seeking mode with the Good Shepherd, please allow Him to become the Lord of all these things. You will seek Him in many places. It takes years to grow but the pain of growth is productive compared to the binding, wretched torture of continuing to live under the old, fetid system.

For the next seventeen years following the reunion with the Good Shepherd, you are living your life in love with Him and growing in grace. But during all of those years, the wall of thorns that has surrounded the sewer hole in our soul has never been cut away to expose the darkest, deepest part. Little Brave Heart remained there, innocent and crying out for freedom as she had been since the day she was banished. Through growth and maturity and life processes, time spent with the Good Shepherd and His word, your heart has been gradually healing. You have believed yourself like little Brave Heart, unworthy of love and good things. You are committed to the Good Shepherd and you attempt to convince yourself that you will remain single and serve only Him, sacrificing marriage and children and yourself once again on the altar of the sick system of family silence, denial and self-righteousness. You find yourself, though, well enough to want to marry, putting it off as long as you could.

It takes all of your manufactured strength you think but His grace enables you to marry an exceptional man and you are blessed with two exceptional children. The stain of guilt and regret stays in the back of your mind constantly though, the remaining residual effects of the trauma and pain. While these happy life events are occurring, the scummy hole deep down has remained locked and hidden, preserving the effects of the putrid brew that has remained alive and fermenting all these years. Untreated pain, shame, guilt and regret have remained buried alive there since the betrayal and abandonment so many years before. Along with little Brave Heart who has been preserved guilt free and pure, yet, imprisoned. She continues to plead for release and the Good Shepherd maintains His loving nudging toward complete freedom in response to her cries. At this stage in your life you are unable to interpret her calling. It is real, true emancipation that was purchased for you and everyone at the cross of Christ. Authenticity is seeking to gain residency in your soul and mind and emotions. Peace with the past beckons you. The Good Shepherd is drawing you to Him once again. Closer. Closer. The stains of guilt and regret, self-hatred and the false beliefs that you maintain about yourself, Brave Heart, cannot live in the same place as His love, mercy, forgiveness and restorative shed blood. His blood spilled at His death paid the price for your freedom, the stripes He bore when He was beaten purchased it for you. (Isaiah 53) This gift is too valuable and priceless not to be taken in and applied to your heart, soul and body, fully.

The lack of identity issues that you have suffered with and that have kept you distracted and tied to the subculture of pain need to be confronted, Brave Heart. Your search for self-worth has disguised itself as service in Christ's name, but in reality, the work done was a substitute, keeping you from being genuine and honest and free from pretense, the very thing that keeps the unprocessed pain hidden. You have perfected the manufactured life, Brave Heart. Even as a lover and follower of the Good Shepherd, you have been able to fool most about your hidden life of pain and shame.

Our true self, little Brave Heart, put away all of this time, nearly forty years, has the self-worth you are seeking and so greatly crave. She has the significance that you long for, unsullied because she belongs to the Good Shepherd. Her identity lies in belonging to Him. She lives in His love even though you put her away, believing her to be evil and shameful because of the evil done to her. It's all been twisted for so long, that you, in your plastic state have lost any awareness and understanding of the truth about her. Herein lies the confusion, the travesty of wrong thinking and wrong believing that has crippled you and succeeded in keeping her hidden. You were deceived into thinking that she was at fault because of what was done to her. The wretched twistedness of believing that the victim is shameful and somehow to blame is a horrible indictment to place upon a child. All of your training and conditioning in pretense and denial as a child has worked well according to the evil intent of the generational system. Your goal was for no one to suspect the evil that had been done. That way, the potential to perpetuate the evil would remain in the scum hole forever. Little did you realize, however, that in spite of the betrayal, the incest and the emotional abandonment, little Brave Heart remained pure and unstained. She belonged to the Good Shepherd. His life was in her. She would never become the same evil that had been done to her. On the other hand, you, young Brave Heart, the impersonator, the imposter, the silent one, was full of potential for chronic self-loathing and everything that it carried along with it. As your protectors all bowed down to the false god of the family system, the door was opened wide for you to fall into many secret ways of maintaining the pretense, thereby harming and hindering our life and potential. As you have grown and lived your life for the nearly forty years since the betrayal, you have perfected the art of living just below the level of the good things that the Good Shepherd had planned for us. The enemy of our soul has made sure to reinforce the false beliefs, so you have only succeeded in dragging your manufactured self nearly into mid-life.

But amazingly, wonderfully, faithfully, little Brave Heart had continued to cry out for freedom. She knew that she was wrongfully imprisoned. She continuously cried for the injustice done to her to be reversed and redeemed. The Good Shepherd was with her in her prison. He had heard her cries and had been nudging you all of our life to listen as well. Stop and listen. He had followed you, urging you, nudging you with His staff, wanting you to set her free. It was in your power to entomb her alive and it was also in your power to open the door to the sewer hole so that He could release her and reunite her with us. It was never His plan for you to hide the best part of us away in that horrid place.

Letter Six

My Dear Brave Heart,

I can see you clearly from here, the Cleft. There is no safer place for you to come to so that you can heal and find your life. Our life. The Father will hide us away, in His presence. He will become the anchor in our soul, our life, our future. The Good Shepherd will lead you here soon, as you walk hand in hand with Him. You will cooperate and work together with the Helper and learn the truth about us. He will be doing his work, as our Michelangelo, chipping away the things in our life and mind and soul that were not meant to have a part in us. The authentic Brave Heart who we were born to be will be revealed and treasured. Freedom is here; it is waiting. It's a progressive process. The full awareness will grow in us that we need to walk successfully and freely. The love and grace that motivates you now to keep moving toward where I am now, will grow in you and you will have the capacity to yield to Him and to participate fully in the work of becoming who we are. Participate fully in the process dear one. Freedom is beckoning you.

Just as the Helper did years before, in 1983, He is now leading you to participate in another missionary trip in 1998, this time to China. Praying for persecuted believers in other countries has been a burden for you, Brave Heart, since 1985. As with the earlier trip to Asia in 1983, this trip also serves as a proverbial "line drawn in the sand" in your walk with Christ, Brave Heart. When you return after three weeks, you are strongly convinced that some significant change must happen. Upon your return home, you are met with the symptoms of "reverse culture shock," a form of unsettledness and discontent with life after witnessing the lives of Christians who often have so little material possessions but a most pure and precious faith and relationship with the Lord Jesus. The beautiful simplicity of what you have experienced clashes mightily with your unresolved issues, Brave Heart. In addition, during that year, your six-year-old son is diagnosed with autism, which only serves to increase the tension in your life, plastic Brave Heart. Gathering all of your emotional energy, you make a serious, sincere cry for change to the Lord. Something must change, in our walk, in our ability to deal with life and our concept of us. Our ability to cope with these new issues only compounds the pain of all of the old issues that you have succeeded in smothering all this time.

Our heart has continued on a healing course, slowly over the last fifteen years, since your reunion with the Good Shepherd but the level of discontent and need is shifting into high gear. Then, an almost unexpected gift comes within a short time after your return from China. Your husband has a job offer out of state, in another region of the country in fact. It will be a fresh start in life at forty. At first you see it as an opportunity for more and different service for yourself Brave Heart. Surely, there must be a good chance of finding your self-worth and self-satisfaction in this new location and hope the ache in your heart and the sensation of strangling will dissipate there.

The new life in a new place begins well for you and your family, Brave Heart. You breathe a breath of fresh air, anticipating good things happening to equip you with new tools and strength to keep the sewer hole covered well as you go on and find a life in spite of what you have carried with you.

Within the course of twenty-four months after the move though, the fresh start has become a series of new trauma mixed with the success that your family finds. Unexpected tragedy brings heartbreak. With your hopes dashed, a season of new struggle begins, compounding your sadness and anger. Doubt and a sense of "what have we done" overtake the seeming promise of a new life.

After the move in 2000, your father is diagnosed in the first week of January 2001 with metastatic cancer. Then your father-in-law dies in February. Your father undergoes treatment and surgery over the next few months but he dies on September 17, 2001. It is a huge heartbreak, Brave Heart. He loved and served the Good Shepherd. He left a legacy of hard work but also a host of unresolved issues that caused a blowup from the inside out—just as it had attempted to do to you twenty-two years earlier, Brave Heart.

He was the patriarch of the subculture of pain and denial, our father. He was born innocent, as we were. He was raised in a perpetual state of chaos, insecurity, lack and neglect. The firstborn son, set up to have the mantle of the subculture fitted to him, at a young age. It was inherited, assumed without question. Who knows how long the mantle has existed and been passed down in a family system where the dysfunction is modeled and dripped down, covering the next generation with the insidious sap of unprocessed pain. Unbelief mixed with belief, alcoholism, enabling, spinning, being used, neglected and abused. Does it sound familiar Brave Heart? Nothing is ever resolved in your father's family of origin. He becomes the patriarch while still a child. Assuming the role of protector and emotional leader that should have never been forced on him. His response to being unjustly saddled with things that no child should bear was to bury the pain underground, his lifelong mode of coping and survival. Thus began the slow burn of anger, disappointment and disillusionment. The undue weight and burden stunted his emotional growth and development. He never truly walked free of the effects of his stolen childhood and continued demand of his original family. The weight of the mantle only increased it. The insidious nature of the mantle of pain maintained its strength by feeding off of the constant supply of unprocessed issues and lack of conflict resolution. The main form of coping and surviving of course became the great Pretense. If the secrets are kept and no one outside the family knows the truth, then it doesn't really matter. If the family is strong enough or sick enough to contain the truth and maintain the front, it must be done at all costs. The family system, the subculture of pride and denial fueled by secrecy, becomes the norm, both inwardly and outwardly. Shame and unprocessed pain are the deadly stimulants, the accelerants of the perversion of the pioneer spirit. Instead of motivating a family to bravery, to move forward into the unknown to break new, fertile ground in order to plant seeds to grow and harvest a healthy crop of believers and followers of Christ, the stubborn independence and isolation of the subculture weakens and constricts any true freedom and growth of families into their destinies.

Brave Heart, can you see that the mantle of pain must be woven to fit the new generation in order that the code of family loyalty will be upheld and passed down despite the costs. There is no official ceremony or ritual of passing down this mantle. As it was with you and I, the key is to get the innocent next in line to assume it by modeling and conditioning them. This causes the wearing of the mantle by the next generation to seem normal, even vital, necessary to keep the precariously dysfunction alive and well, maintained by seemingly normal, hardworking people that are bereft emotionally and could never admit to it.

This was our legacy, Brave Heart. From the patriarch of pain came a propensity for self-loathing caused by a dramatic lack of identity: a byproduct but necessary component of the subculture. Pride and denial fueled by secrets and unprocessed pain, trauma and conflict, all covered over by an insidious coat of shame. It's the perfect combination to prohibit and limit the satisfaction and joy and true purpose in life. It's not what the Creator intended our lives to be.

This is what opened the door and made you vulnerable as a child, Brave Heart. This inherited system is just dripping with the slime of shame. You were a prime target for incest. A first-born child, destined to assume the mantle. A child with no firm identity established early on. You were longing for attention. Left alone with evil and unprotected by those who were preoccupied by their own deep levels of pain, using all of their energy just to keep their own heads above water. They were so absorbed that they didn't hear or ignored the voice of the Good Shepherd, who I am positive tried to warn them my dear young, plastic Brave Heart.

Where was the Good Shepherd? He was there. As it says in Genesis 1:1-3, the presence of the Lord was not removed by the presence of darkness. The perpetuator chose to execute his free will to do evil. With no resistance, it happened again, three or four more times. We were forever changed but never guilty, Brave Heart. As in the Garden of Eden, our eyes were opened to the reality of sin and perversion and multiple adult issues that our childish heart and psyche wasn't ready to process. Just as in the Garden, you covered over the real little Brave Heart and you became afraid, ashamed. We survived the trauma physically but the psychological and emotional effects as well as the continued emotional abandonment set us on a path of self-loathing and desperate self-sufficiency, isolating and severely limiting us. Somehow, you sensed that any confession of the horror would be a betrayal and cause an upheaval in our family. That was when you began the assumption of the mantle of pain, carrying it to protect the subculture in the family system. Thus was born in us the burden to keep the secrets intact—and eventually to keep true, innocent little Brave Heart buried as well.

You were assisted in forming and maintaining your veiled, secret life by the perpetuator of the subculture of pain. This person contributes to the maintenance of the dysfunctional functioning of the family system by making sure it continues indefinitely. This perpetuator prolongs the existence of the subculture by denying the symptoms of sexual and emotional abuse and neglect that arise and show themselves periodically, especially during stressful times. The team of the patriarch and the perpetuator, and father and the maintainer, are two people who are so consumed and weighed down by the bulk of the mantle, that they never trust enough to allow the subculture to be blasted apart by the healing power of the truth. Keeping the family sewer hole covered and its contents buried alive inside the family loyalty system guarantees it maintenance and continued ability to hinder the lives and destinies of so many and so much potential. The truth. It could change the future of generations. Instead, the mantle of pain is passed and expected to be carried without question into the next branch of the family tree. It's an unholy setup, Brave Heart. It's not what the Good Shepherd had planned for them. Or for us.

The death of the patriarch brings more confusion and desperation. It's now up to you, Brave Heart, to wear the mantle of pain and shame. It is assumed that you must continue on with the caretaking of the subculture of pride and denial. The struggle becomes overwhelming. There is a breakdown in your marriage. Midlife stressors begin to manifest themselves, in both you and your husband. You make one last attempt at running fast and hard, taking your children back to where it all started, to your Egypt. Only there you find a brick wall, a hindrance to your returning to live. There is no other choice now. The Good Shepherd has been offering you a new choice, a new horizon, a new beginning in the midst of the new beginning. It becomes time, really, becomes time, past time to listen to His voice once again and comply. It's only for our good.

You can't balance it all anymore, Brave Heart, with only your plastic front and strength. The lid on the sewer hole is hidden and tightly covered but it takes too much energy and time to uphold the secrecy and to abide by the system. The mantle of shame is too heavy now. It really always was but now your arms and life are full with an exceptional husband and two exceptional children. You can't continue your quest for significance and freedom and self-love this way anymore. Avoiding and running from the arms of the Good Shepherd really has become a worn out ruse. Punishing yourself with loathing and self-condemnation has become so hindering and counterproductive in light of what you know about His love and freedom. It's past time to let go and let yourself drown in the love and redemption of Christ. His everlasting arms are wide open. Always.

You need to admit that you need help; you need to ask for help. It is the cardinal sin against the structure of the subculture of pride and denial. It breaks every code of the system and threatens its very existence. But you have got to turn! Stop pretending! Stop trying to cover the pain and the real issues with more and more busyness and more Christian work and doing. The Good Shepherd has a new choice for you. A new horizon, a true new beginning in the midst of the new beginning that has gone sour.

In this new horizon you can stop pretending and stop avoiding the real, root issues. The climate in your life is ripe for a cataclysmic, phenomenal deliverance. The Helper is there, motivating it, instigating it and leading you to it. You are forty-four years old and at the end of your proverbial rope. You can't balance your life, your marriage, your children's needs and keep the lid clamped down hard on the sewer hole anymore. There isn't enough energy left in you to try to control and protect the subculture of pain. It just isn't working anymore. It has never been so apparent that you need to give up, all of it.

Finally, in November of 2004, you decide to cooperate with the Helper, who only wants good for us, and you ask for His help. You break the code of silence. You find a professional friend, one who loves Christ herself and is dedicated to helping people with the messiness and grittiness of life. Here is where the pain really will start to end, where your claim to authenticity will begin.

There in that safe place, with that safe person, you finally admit to the existence of the sewer hole itself, thereby exposing to the light, the putridness that has been brewing for so many years. It is finally exposed to the awesome scouring power of the Blood of Jesus Christ! The taint and stain that has been so harmful is released to Him, the Master of the Universe, the Redeemer. You open the lid and you give it all to Him, the scum and the filth that has clung to you all this time. You need to proceed now, Brave Heart, into recovery. The cobwebs will clear. From our mind, our emotions, our responses and our reactions. He will bring us into a place of firm foundation. No more swimming in the strong current of old pain, gaining no ground, just carried along by life. The forces in our scarred soul have tried to control the rudder of our life but the Good Shepherd is in charge now. We will learn to live intently, with an eternal perspective, Brave Heart. It will change everything.

The Good Shepherd has brought us to a place where we can make new choices, choices that were unavailable while we lived under the code of the family system. When you opened up that day in the counselor's office, it broke the power of the lies, the power of the subculture in our life. There is a fear of the unknown in letting go of the pretense after all of this time, we were conditioned to believe that this ungodly and pathetic way of life was absolutely necessary and vital to our existence but the fear is unmatched in comparison to the freedom that comes immediately when the fabricated and well maintained system of lies is opened up for examination and expulsion.

Letter Seven

Rock of Ages, cleft for me, let me hide myself in Thee.
Augustus Toplady/Thomas Hastings Isaiah 26:4

The entrance to the Cleft is through the office of that Christ-loving, professional friend that you go to dear one. That is where you will enter the safe place. You will finally pry open the sewer hole in that safe place. You must now work together with the safe friend and the Helper so that all of the putridness that has been brewing for so many years is fully exposed to the awesome cleansing power of the Blood of Jesus Christ. The effects in our soul will be undone. You will let our Michelangelo work, chipping away all of the falseness that you have been living in, secretly. Your behavior will change as you no longer live in reaction to the charges that you held against yourself and little Brave Heart.

As your time in the Cleft develops, the seeming isolation and seclusion will become vital to you as you heal.

The power of the love of the Good Shepherd and your confidence in it and Him is what will change you, will keep you there. The old coping system will be replaced with authenticity and more and more freedom. This is the product and result of gaining and living in the truth of who the Good Shepherd is and who you are in Him, because we have always belonged to Him, just like little Brave Heart. Our identity will be established. Security will accompany the knowledge of who you are and whom you belong to. This will bring the greatest level of freedom and the greatest joy.

Brave Heart, we are well on the way of coming out of victimhood! Soon we won't just be a survivor but a thriving overcomer. He will redeem all of the things that happened and threatened to end your life. We will now grow in grace and peace. We belong to Him. We will continually unlearn the harmful things. We will never again be buried by filth and perverseness will never suffocate or freeze you from your real life. Many stones will be removed from our soul, the evidence left from the huge glacier of the family system that tried to flatten us. What is left after the rock picking done by the Helper will be fertile soil, tilled for the seeds of His love to grow and bear fruit that will remain. We will love others and our self from a right place with right motives. The peace, joy and contentment you will find in the Cleft will never leave you now. Our Father, the Rock of Ages, has made a place in Himself that is fit only for us Brave Heart. The dysfunctional family system that strove to keep its unholy tentacles embedded deeply in our soul and mind has had its power broken because you broke the code of silence.

When you first enter the Cleft, we won't have a full understanding or awareness of what we need. Recovery isn't in your thought process yet. You are desperate for relief from the pain... all of the pain that has seeped out of the sewer hole and wedged itself into the corners of our soul. There are leftover effects of trauma that has only been skimmed over and then dumped into the gravel pit, the annex to the sewer hole. When the Redeemer is allowed full access to the scummy brew that has become infected, the power of His love and redemption will dry up and blast away the guilt, self-condemnation and regret. You also will release yourself, and little Brave Heart, of all charges. The sense of destiny that belongs to little Brave Heart will be restored and renewed. Our legacy will become light, life, hope, peace and eternal freedom. It's been waiting for us. The choice to make now Brave Heart is the level of commitment that you will make to the Helper. Yielding to the voice and hand of the Michelangelo, is absolutely essential, the key component to our continued progression in the cleft. Be encouraged in the long season of unlearning and re-learning how to be motivated by His love and how not to be driven by our insecurity and pain. Keep walking forward with your hand in His, even if it means wading back through the deep pool of pain. It has no power over you now. Not when the Good Shepherd is charge of it all. The gnawing ache in our Heart and soul will dissipate and transform into a confident trust. A solid place to live with eternity in view. Our new professional friend will be there too, faithfully, fully for us.

Dearest Brave Heart, the Cleft is your safe place, your refuge. We are now in the Father's hand. The Rock of Ages made a space in Him and put us there when you asked for help. It is a haven for the serious processing that we need to undergo. At first, you won't recognize it as such but as our Michelangelo, the Helper, does His work, we will come to understand it. He wants to chip away all of those things that have accumulated in your soul that weren't meant to be a part of us. He will bring the masterpiece in us to light. The person that Brave Heart was created to be will be revealed. He will work through the compilation of the evil that was piled upon us, to hinder us, to negate our mission. As we make progress, with the assistance of the Helper and His assistant, the professional friend, we will come to love the work they are doing, we are doing. The loving hands are crafting you and the subculture of pain that drove us will be chipped away and become null and void. It will no longer drive our life and the pretense that kept it alive will die off as well. The guilt, regret and self-loathing will dry up and become non-factors in our life. The lack of power to be true to our self and the inability to accept the unconditional love of the Good Shepherd for our self will no longer hinder us. We will shed the sense that we have disqualified ourselves from the good things that the Good Shepherd has planned for us. The fact that the stain of guilt has been eradicated from our soul will become a living reality for us. This will all come by faith and trust in the Helper as He brings you through the process in the Cleft over the course of time. The old twisted and ineffective coping mechanisms and the secret system will fade and fall off, away from us, like a growth whose blood supply has been cut off.

Our heart and soul are on the road to permanent healing but there is one significant piece missing yet Brave Heart. You, the formerly plastic Brave Heart, created to impersonate little Brave Heart, the real, innocent part of us is still hiding something. The sewer hole has been exposed and the chipping away of the effects of trauma and betrayal has commenced, but where is she? After we have spent some significant time in the Cleft, we have been healing consistently. It is only after a certain amount of healing has been obtained by us that we make a dramatic realization. Little Brave Heart is still imprisoned in the sewer hole. Even with the door standing wide open. She has been crying out all this time, aching to be released so that she can join the Good Shepherd and us in a sweet re-union! Over the course of time, with our hand in the hand of the Good Shepherd, we have really faced the truth and with our confidence and faith in His ability, we are able to place all of the trauma, the horror, the abandonment, and the betrayal into His hands at last. He will, because of who He is, redeem all of the deeds, shame, guilt, regret and self-hatred that have plagued us for so long. We are beginning to be free, really free. As these layers are dealt with and removed forever, He is able to bring us back to where the pain originated. This is where we find little Brave Heart, in the place where you banished her so long ago. She is unchanged though, she is still the pure and innocent little girl that loved and belonged to the Good Shepherd. What we have failed to realize until now, until so much of the pain has been removed, is that she is still there, waiting for us to release her. The Good Shepherd has been nudging us all along, to remind us where she was but we couldn't see it until now. Until the layers of pain were no longer clouding our vision. Until we had given up and stopped using the evil tool of denial to try to navigate our way through life. We were once drowning in deep, murky waters, Brave Heart, before we came to the Cleft but now he has pulled us up and out and is washing away the muck and chipping away the hardness of the stone. Then, one day, suddenly, we see her. Little Brave Heart, the pure, innocent part of us, the golden part is there still, in the pit where she doesn't belong. She was born to grow, develop and flourish in the love of the Good Shepherd, where we are now, Brave Heart. Her potential to grow into a remarkable image of the Good Shepherd has been preserved. She never lost an ounce of her potential when she was locked away for so long, unlawfully. We tried for years to ignore her cries but now we can hear her. The shock of the realization of what we have done to her is devastating at first but we have come far enough in our recovery that we now have the courage to go and get her. We have lived as though freedom was unattainable but the fact that she is alive, intact, strong and determined to proceed with her life shocks us and motivates us to go and get her and bring her home to us. We have faced what we have been running from, Brave Heart, our own true self, our core, our identity and we have brought her back. Forever. Our legacy will be forever changed from the plastic future we thought we had to manufacture to survive. We are beginning to understand the power and purpose of the Cleft, Brave Heart. It is becoming less of a physical place and more of a living, breathing place where we will live eternally.

Little Brave Heart knew all along that she was wrongfully imprisoned. She continuously cried for the injustice done to her to be reversed and redeemed. The Good Shepherd had heard her and had been with her along, sustaining her. He had also been nudging you all along, urging you gently with His staff, wanting you to set you free. It was in your power to entomb her alive and it was also in your power to open the door to the sewer hole so that He could reunite her with us. It was never the Father's plan for you to place the best part of yourself away in a place where only shame and perversity would dwell. He is only good and He only wants our good and He wants Christ, the Good Shepherd to receive all the glory.

Being reunited with little Brave Heart now of course brings new meaning to the word wholeness for us, Brave Heart. We are all together believing the way the Good Shepherd does about us. We are growing into our worth and value since little Brave Heart joined us. We are learning new ways of believing and living the truth about our self and what the Good Shepherd has in mind for us. We are really dealing with our issues instead of ignoring and denying them. Sometimes, we must grab the hand of the Good Shepherd again as He walks us back thru some mucky, painful water where we had been drowning before we came to the Cleft. We are really facing the truth, about all of it and we are now able, together, to place all of the trauma, pain, abandonment and betrayal into His hands at last. We are becoming free, really free, as little Brave Heart always has been.

When you step into the Cleft and our recovery is initiated, you soon realize that you have taken a giant leap toward true freedom and that there is no going back. For two full years, you continue to meet with the committed Christ follower, your professional friend, your counselor, and your therapist. There is no shame in asking for help

Beloved Reader. All help and healing originates with the Creator, and He has given gifts to His believers so that they are enabled to extend His hand and His help to anyone who seeks it.

When your friend departs, you find yourself on a new plateau of emotional health. As you continue the healing process with the assistance of the Helper and one or two listening, safe friends, you continue to sort through and face issues that before were ignored and/or buried. Slowly but surely, you are changing your thinking, mostly about yourself. You are beginning to believe the way the Good Shepherd does about us. You are finding our worth and value. You are unlearning many untruths. You are beginning to learn a new type of work. It's a resting work, a trusting work. It is the work that Jesus talked about in John 6:27-29. This scripture is becoming one of your life's verses. Continue cooperating with the Helper, the Holy Spirit, and the presence of God in the Earth. This is why you came to the Cleft, to learn to fully cooperate with the Helper, in love, not out of compulsion or fear. The process of recovery in our soul will make room for little Brave Heart to begin to grow and mature and to be restored as the person we were created to be. Allow the Helper to do His chipping of the marble, removing everything that isn't us. The masterpiece that we are will be shaped and revealed. The real Brave Heart can live fully and authentically. As a new creation in Christ, little Brave Heart can now flourish. Of course, this means that in reality, as little Brave Heart grows and matures in her relationship with the Good Shepherd and lives out His plan, plastic, manufactured Brave Heart must pass away. Indeed, we are already dead. (See 2 Corinthians 5:17.) The new person that she is becoming now that she has been freed is growing up into me, the one and only Brave Heart, living in the Cleft, in His hands. I am living now in freedom. There is still work to be done in my soul, young Brave Heart, but I am gaining more awareness and surety every day. I am unlearning the harmful ways of thinking and living that you held onto for so long after you banished little Brave Heart to the sewer hole. I have found the grace and the time and the effective way to grieve our losses. The loss of our childhood, our innocence, any authenticity in relationships and most of all, the love and self-respect that was corroded in us. I can now fall into the everlasting arms of the Good Shepherd and rest in His powerful, merciful and all-encompassing love. There is no more resisting or stiff-arming Him. No more lying or pretending. To yourself or anyone else. We were a victim of incest and the system of shame, self-hatred, shame and silence. The purpose of the trauma, the incest, the secrecy was to steal little Brave Heart's life and destiny away. The evil done to her was designed to get her to live her life as a substitute, manufacturing it as she went along. You fell into the trap young Brave Heart, as you were conditioned to do. Young Brave

Heart, you were supposed to stay broken and embittered and faking it all along the wrong path. If the false plan had succeeded, with her locked away, her God-given destiny would have remained locked up with her. But you yielded, young Brave Heart, to the hand of mercy. We are now in the Cleft, where our Michelangelo has been sculpting an overcomer, a victor because you changed your mind. You yielded. We gave up the boatload of pain that was impossible to bear and remain alive. We needed time and honesty, caring and loving reinforcement of the truth. We needed time to identify the pain, buried for so long under many layers of pretense. We needed to recognize the disconnect in our soul so that we could reunite little Brave Heart with the older version of herself. A healthy version: honest and transparent, free to love our self, the good as well as the flaws, with Eternity in view. We recognized and reconciled with little Brave Heart. The justified anger that you nursed has plagued us. It is dissipating now and is being replaced with the understanding and compassion that little Brave Heart is growing into. She is becoming the person that the Father intended her to be. It will be an eternal process, this developing into Christlikeness, but He is patiently and gracefully at work. Our work is to believe Him and in the One who sent Him. Our legacy will be emotional health. Little Brave Heart had it all along. The sewer hole couldn't steal it away from her. She knew the Good Shepherd and she knew that she belonged to

Him. This is the motivating force in her life. It is the foundation of her life and her existence. That is why she could never be truly put away and silenced. She was never shame or what was done to her. Her heart and soul were golden and fixed in Him. She was His forever. His job was to reconcile her with us, Brave Heart, and with Himself. He would never let her go. Only the evil done to her separated her from us. She was never that evil. Those in charge of her failed her. The Good Shepherd never did.

All of this that I am sharing with you, young Brave Heart, comes from my perspective in and from the Cleft, the safe place in Him to heal and to live. He fit you into this place and it surrounded you on all sides. As we live and grow into our destiny, Brave Heart, always remember to listen to the voice of the Helper. He will continue His sculpting process, continually making us into a likeness of Christ, the Good Shepherd. Eventually, that likeness will serve as a compass, pointing toward the love and life that is waiting for everyone, whether they choose to come to know and believe Him or they don't. This is the power of a transformed life, Brave Heart. To go from living encased in the marble of our humanity to the allowing of the "David," the likeness of Jesus Christ, to draw others into His embrace so that they can know His love and the beauty of His redemption.

Live and love on, Brave Heart. You are the one that was rescued and removed from an unjust judgment and jail. You are standing on a firm foundation now and your life is founded on the truth. There is no greater destiny than your life in Him. It is everlasting. Live and love on. We are His ambassadors and our mission is reconciliation. Brave Heart has always been a missionary from the start. Always remember that on and during every mission, everywhere we go, His intent is always to do more within us than through us. It's the highest goal and purpose in the universe, my beloved Brave Heart. And so it will be also for our children and grandchildren. We have shed the mantle of pain. Forever.

Continue on with the process in the Cleft, dear Brave Heart. The desire to fill the emptiness and to eliminate the pain is what brought you here. That drive will develop eventually into a mature love and relationship with the Good Shepherd. We loved Him as a child, before the betrayal. You returned to Him as a young adult and you followed Him, seeking relief in mid-life. As more of the marble is chipped away, what remains is that we will be simply more and deeply in love with the Good Shepherd. That love will carry us forward into the transforming process of discipleship. He has showed us who He is and who we are. We will never again limp our way through life, wounded to the core.

Afterword

Beloved,

I pray that you may prosper in every way and that your body may keep well, even as I know your soul keeps well and prospers. 3 John 2

I see you, young Brave Heart, from my view, my home, our home, here in the Cleft. Because of the faithfulness of the Good Shepherd, you are on your way here and soon we will live always in the freedom of His love, reunited with little Brave Heart at last. The seasons in your life will change as you make your way here but the grace you need to live well will never depart from you.

With the Good Shepherd as the Captain of our life, we will change our legacy. Our friendship with the Helper will blossom with fruitfulness and we will witness little Brave Heart, His masterpiece, grow into her destiny, our destiny. We will come to understand that our "greatest work" will be to believe in Jesus Christ and the One who sent Him. We will live out the mission in our soul, our ambassadorship. This is what our little Brave Heart was crying out for when she was locked away. We will walk and live out the liberty that she possessed from the beginning and we will be His sent ones.

Most importantly, we will never fit our children or grandchildren with the insidious, toxic mantle of loyalty to a system of secrecy that perpetuates harmful generational idolatry that would bind, restrict and separate them from the Good Shepherd and His loving destiny for them. They will know Him and the fullness of His love, without restraint.

When the Good Shepherd brought little Brave Heart out of the sewer hole, He sent her, running to find us, to meet us and to be reunited with us forever. Then He turned and destroyed the dungeon in our soul. The power of His finished, redemptive work sealed forever by His shed blood, totally obliterated that hole in our soul along with every trace of guilt and shame. It is all gone, as far as the east is from the west. Forever.

I love you young Brave Heart. I'm here in the Cleft waiting for you and for little Brave Heart. Our reunion will be complete and eternal. I could write forever about His peace and love and about who He is. Perhaps someday I will. Until then, always keep your eyes fixed on the

Good Shepherd and never stop listening to the Helper. Come on and keep coming.

Love always,
Your Brave Heart

Dear Reader,

If your heart has been wounded, if you have been betrayed or been made a victim of sexual molestation, incest or rape, please know that just as Brave Heart found her life and peace and healing, it is available to you as well. Please find a helpful, supportive listener, friend or counselor. There is no good reason not to tell someone. You are far too valuable and precious to suffer the betrayal and then to suffer in silence. The Good Shepherd is real and He is the Lord. He knows you and He loves you. He suffered so that you could prosper and be in health, both physical and emotional health. He died so that you could freely live out His good plan for your life. Invite Him in, ask Him to help you. He will never leave you or fail you.

Blessings and peace,
Your Brave Heart

If you or someone you know has been a victim of any form of sexual abuse or is struggling with suicidal thoughts and depression please contact a trusted friend or a professional.

I personally know and trust these two women. They are compassionate, Christ loving counselors:

Anna Raab M.A. Counseling
Board Certified Neurofeedback
2530 E 71st Suite M Tulsa, OK 74136
(918) 933-4455 · *abundantlivingneuro.com*

Adrienne Owens Monroe PhD. LCSW
Certified Christian Counselor, Certified Sexual Education
Therapist Licensed, Ordained Minister
6977 Nexus Court Suite 104 Fayetteville, NC 28304
(910) 229 8437 · *peaceofmindbodyspirit@gmail.com*